PUBLISH

Julie Brooke

Copyright © 2019 All rights reserved.

No part of this publication may be copied, reproduced in any format, by any means, electronic or otherwise, without prior consent from the copyright owner and publisher of this book.

Contents

Introduction 4

Apple and Cinnamon Mug Cake 12

Bacon and Cheese Mug 13

Baileys Chocolate Mug Cake 14

Banana Mug Cake 15

Blondie Mug Cake 16

Blueberry Mug Cake 17

Carrot Cake and Cream Cheese Mug Cake 18

Champagne Mug Cake 20

Cheddar and Bacon Mug Cake 22

Cherry Mug Cake 23

Choc Chip Cookie Dough Mug Cake 25

Chocolate Almond Mug Cake 26

Chocolate Mug Cake 27

Chocolate Orange Mug Cake 28

Chocolate Peanut Butter Mug Cake 30

Chocolate Zucchini Mug Cake 31

Cinnamon Mug Cake 32

Coconut Mug Cake 34

Coffee Mug Cake 35

Cookies and Cream Mug Cake 36

Doughnut Mug Cake 37

Eggnog Mug Cake 38

French Toast Mug Cake 39

Funfetti Mug Cake 40

Guinness Mug Cake 41

Honey Mug Cake 43

Ice Cream Mug Cake 44

Lemon Mug Cake 45

Matcha Mug Cake 46

Mint Chocolate Mug Cake 47

Mocha Mug Cake 48

Nutella Indulgence Mug Cake 50

Oatmeal and Raisin Mug Cake 51

Peach Mug Cake 52

Peanut Butter and Jelly Mug Cake 53

Pear and Almond Mug Cake 54

Pecan Chocolate Chip Mug Cake 55

Pizza Mug 56

Pumpkin Mug Cake 57

Rainbow Mug Cake 58

Raspberry Mug Cake 59

Red Velvet Mug Cake 60

Rum Mug Cake 61

S'Mores Mug Cake 62

Salted Caramel Mug Cake 63

Strawberries with Cream Mug Cake 64

Triple Chocolate Mug Cake 65

Vanilla Chai Mug Cake 67

Vanilla Mug Cake 68

White Chocolate and Cranberry Mug Cake 70

Introduction

What can be more appealing to any food lover than the idea of a two-minute cake? Two minutes to create a wonderfully delicious, warm and beautiful cake might seem impossible. However, with mug cakes and this book full of recipes, you can do exactly that.

There are many benefits to the mug cake. It requires very little equipment. The quantities needed are far less. The cleaning-up takes seconds. Yet in two minutes, you can produce a wonderful cake in a mug, that is a true delight and pleasure for one.

If you love baking but find yourself lacking in time and not wanting to waste ingredients on a large cake that may not get eaten, then the mug cake is the perfect solution for you. If you want the fastest and easiest treat possible for yourself or your family, then you will love the mug cake.

The mug cake can be a little masterpiece with stunning flavor combinations and melting chocolate surprises contained inside. It is still a homemade cake, made with real ingredients, but takes hardly any time to create and has no waste. It is the ideal treat that can be on the table literally in minutes and will become a family favorite even faster!

This book holds 50 of the very best mug cake recipes to be found. They can all be created with little more than a mug and your microwave and they take less than two minutes to cook. You will find a huge variety of mug cakes inside including even a couple of savory mug cakes that make a perfect breakfast or brunch.

Just before you start cooking, do read my top mug cake tips over the following pages. They will save you time and let you get the best possible results as quickly as you can.

Enjoy reading this collection of mug cake recipes. By the end, you will be a mug cake expert, able to create a warming and delicious treat for yourself, your friends and your family in under two minutes every time!

Happy mug cake making!

Julie

Equipment

One of the many great things about mug cakes is that you need so little equipment. You need a mug, a microwave, tablespoons and a fork to mix all the ingredients together. That's it! No need to store lots of unnecessary equipment that can gather dust and take up wasted space. No need for lots of washing up or any cleaning.

Your mug cake will be ready to eat in minutes and the clean-up is minimal!

Ingredients

Mug cakes are just smaller versions of full-size homemade cakes, so it is no surprise they use the same ingredients, just far less of them. Here are a few points about specific ingredients.

Butter – assume when the recipes talk about butter, that it is unsalted. Most of the recipes in this book call for butter. You can substitute oil if you prefer of course but be careful not to add too much. I have found an excessive amount will make the cake take on a rather rubbery texture.

Flour – All-purpose flour or plain flour is used in all recipes unless stated otherwise.

Sugar – Most of these recipes use sugar. Unless otherwise stated, this should be assumed to be white. For some recipes, brown sugar will go better, and I have put down brown sugar clearly. Do feel use to use a sugar substitute in these recipes if preferred.

Salt – Some of these recipes use a tiny bit of salt – never more than a pinch. When mentioned, table salt should be used.

Vanilla – the majority of these recipes call for vanilla extract. It can vary from a ¼ of a teaspoon up to a full teaspoon for particular recipes. I find vanilla goes beautifully in just about any mug cake.

Chocolate Chips – in many recipes there are mini chocolate chips which are assumed to be semi-sweet. Feel free to adapt to dark chocolate or white if you prefer.

Milk – many of these recipes call for milk. You can use whatever milk suits your fancy or dietary needs. I have tried many of these with almond or coconut milk for example and been pleased with the results.

Top 6 Mug Cake Making Tips

Here are my personal top tips for creating a beautiful mug cake for yourself or friends and family every time.

Tip 1

Understand how your microwave works. By this I mean you will need a few attempts to figure out exactly how powerful your microwave is and for how long you should be cooking your mug cake. Most microwaves will be anywhere from 800 to 1200 or even more watts in power. The recipes in this book assume you are using an 800-watt microwave. If you have a more powerful model, you can choose to lower the power slightly or just cook for a little less time. Rather than a minute and 30 seconds, try 50 seconds and then go up in 10 second increments until you find the perfect time.

Don't worry if you don't get it right first time. A little experimentation will soon lead to the best results. Every microwave is slightly different, but these recipes can be made in any microwave you have. The desired outcome is a rich, moist, gooey mug cake.

Tip 2

Choose the right size and shape of mug. This is an important one. You need a mug that is firstly microwave-safe. After that, think about the size of mug you need. I tend to go for larger to avoid spillage if the ingredients overflow. I also like the mugs to be a uniform, cylindrical shape. If they have a small base and become larger as they become taller, the cake will not cook evenly. Try and avoid very tall mugs. They are usually thinner than a standard mug making it difficult for even cooking.

Make sure your mug has a firm handle. The mug will get hot during the cooking process and you don't want to hurt your hands if grasping it without a handle.

This book is all about "mug" cakes, but don't let that stop you using any other container you like of course. You can try anything that is safe in the microwave.

Tip 3

Avoid overfilling. Not only do you run the risk of spillage in the microwave leading to a time-consuming clean-up, there is the added risk of your mug cracking or even disintegrating entirely. Try filling up your mug to just beyond the half way point to begin with and see how far the cake rises. You can always make two mugs or simply use a larger vessel if appropriate.

When first starting out however, I would choose the biggest mug you can find. This will give you a clear idea about how far the ingredients will rise without worrying about spillage. You can always tweak the quantities later.

Tip 4

Mixing your ingredients. When making a full-size cake, this can be quite an exhausting process. It is much easier of course with the smaller quantities needed for mug cakes, but nevertheless, it is an important step. Give all the ingredients a good mix with a fork and ensure you get all the mixture, even at the base of the mug.

Tip 5

Mug cakes need to be eaten quickly. Once you leave them for a while, they will harden and become more or less inedible. They must be consumed quickly once out the oven. This is never a problem as they go very quickly, but unlike a standard cake, mug cakes can't be kept for any length of time. They will not last overnight.

They may be very hot coming out of the microwave, especially with a gooey center, however they should be eaten after a minute of cooling at most.

Tip 6

Decorating. I have made quite a few suggestions for toppings of your mug cake in the recipes below, however feel free to adapt the topping with your personal and family favorites. As mug cakes are individual by their very nature, they give everyone the perfect opportunity to have exactly the topping they like.

Encourage family and guests to get involved if not with the cooking, then certainly with decorating their own mug cake once it is cooked.

I very much hope you will enjoy the many different mug cake recipes in this book. They have proved immensely popular with friends and family over decades and I am so delighted and honored to have the opportunity to share them with you now.

Next time you have a spare minute, bring out this book with your favorite mug and create your own mug cake mini-masterpiece!

Apple and Cinnamon Mug Cake

Ingredients

1 tablespoon butter

1 egg

3 tablespoons flour

2 tablespoon sugar

¼ teaspoon baking powder

3 tablespoons milk

½ teaspoon cinnamon

2 tablespoons apple, diced

Instructions

Add the butter to a mug and melt in the microwave for 20 seconds. Add the egg and whisk. Add in the flour, sugar, baking powder, milk and cinnamon and mix well. Fold in the diced apple. Cook in the microwave for 1 minute and 30 seconds, dust the top with a little more cinnamon and serve.

Bacon and Cheese Mug

Pizza in a mug? Absolutely yes and it tastes beautiful. If you need an immediate pizza hit, then this recipe is perfect and takes 2 minutes!

Ingredients

4 tablespoons flour

¼ teaspoon baking powder

Pinch of salt

1 tablespoon butter

3 tablespoons milk

1 tablespoon cheddar cheese, grated

1 tablespoon bacon

Instructions

Add the flour, baking powder, salt and butter into a mug and mix well. Add the milk, cheese and bacon and mix again until everything is combined. Cook in the microwave for 1 minute and serve.

Baileys Chocolate Mug Cake

Bailey's Irish Cream goes perfectly with chocolate. Try it once for St Patrick's Day and you'll be making it all year!

Ingredients

1 tablespoon butter

4 tablespoons flour

2 tablespoons sugar

1 teaspoon oil

½ teaspoon baking powder

1 tablespoon cocoa powder, unsweetened

Pinch of salt

3 tablespoons milk

½ teaspoon vanilla

2 tablespoons Baileys Irish Cream

Instructions

Melt the butter in the microwave for 20 seconds. Add in the milk, oil, vanilla and Baileys and whisk together. Add the flour, sugar, baking powder, salt and cocoa powder and mix well. Cook in the microwave for 1 minute 30 seconds, allow to cool slightly and serve.

Banana Mug Cake

This goes so well with a huge number of added extras. I've provided the essential base recipe below, but I have also tried adding chocolate chips, walnuts, pecans, almonds, raisins and peanut butter for great combinations. Try them all and your own ideas to see which is the most popular!

Ingredients

1 tablespoon butter

4 tablespoons flour

¼ teaspoon baking powder

½ teaspoon vanilla

2 tablespoons sugar, brown

1 egg

2 tablespoons milk

1 banana, mashed

Instructions

Melt the butter for 20 seconds in a mug. Add in the egg, milk and vanilla and whisk well. Add the flour, sugar and baking powder and mix. Fold in the banana and any optional extras you like. Cook in the microwave for 1 minute and 30 seconds and serve.

Blondie Mug Cake

If you take away the chocolate from a brownie, then you have a blondie! This is a fun, fast recipe which always proves a great treat.

Ingredients

1 tablespoon butter

4 tablespoons flour

½ teaspoon baking powder

3 tablespoons milk

½ teaspoon vanilla

1 tablespoon white chocolate chips

Instructions

Melt the butter in a mug in a microwave for 20 seconds. Add the flour, baking powder, milk and vanilla and mix together. Fold in the white chocolate chips. Cook in the microwave for 1 minute and 30 seconds. Remove to cool a little and serve.

Blueberry Mug Cake

Fresh blueberries are better for this but frozen works extremely well. This is a light and beautiful looking mug cake which works well for breakfast.

Ingredients

2 tablespoons butter

4 tablespoons flour

¼ teaspoon baking powder

2 tablespoons sugar

1 egg

Pinch of salt

½ teaspoon cinnamon

2 tablespoons milk

1 teaspoon vanilla

2 tablespoons blueberries

Instructions

Melt the butter in a mug for 20 seconds in the microwave. Add in the egg with the vanilla and milk and whisk. Now add in the flour, baking powder, sugar, cinnamon and salt and mix well. Fold in the blueberries. Cook in the microwave for 1 minute and 30 seconds. Sprinkle with a little sugar and serve.

Carrot Cake and Cream Cheese Mug Cake

The drizzled cream cheese over the top of the mug cake just as it comes out the microwave really makes this cake for me. I love the taste of carrots and the extra in all my cakes and the taste goes perfectly with the nutmeg and cinnamon in this mu cake as well.

Ingredients

4 tablespoons flour

¼ teaspoon baking powder

1 tablespoon butter

2 tablespoons milk

1 tablespoons sugar, brown

½ teaspoon cinnamon

¼ teaspoon nutmeg

2 tablespoon carrots, shredded

1 tablespoon cream cheese

1 teaspoon powdered sugar

1 teaspoon water

Chopped walnuts

Instructions

Melt the butter in the mug in the microwave. Add the flour, nutmeg, baking powder, sugar, vanilla and cinnamon and mix together. Add in the carrots and mix again. Cook in the microwave for 1 minute and 30 seconds. Add the cream cheese, powdered sugar and water together and mix. Add a little more water if too thick or a little more sugar if too runny. Drizzle over the mug cake, place the chopped walnuts on top and serve.

Champagne Mug Cake

These are great for that special occasion and look amazing in a proper fluted glass. Add a little frosting on the top and it's the perfect complement to the real thing.

The ideal birthday or New Year's Eve celebration mug cake!

Ingredients

1 tablespoon butter

4 tablespoons flour

2 tablespoons sugar

½ teaspoon baking powder

Pinch of salt

2 tablespoons milk

2 tablespoons champagne

1 teaspoon oil

Topping

2 tablespoons butter

1 tablespoon champagne

4 tablespoons powdered sugar

Instructions

Melt the butter in a mug for 20 seconds. Add the flour, sugar, salt, baking powder and mix well. Add the milk, champagne and oil and whisk together. Fill a champagne flute glass about half way up and add to the microwave for 1 minute.

Make the frosting by adding the ingredients together and beating until all is light and fluffy. Pipe onto the cake in the glass and add a little glitter for that flamboyant touch. You can also make a pink champagne version by adding just a little food coloring into the mix above before cooking.

Cheddar and Bacon Mug Cake

If you fancy a quick, warming and delicious breakfast or brunch snack, then this is the one for you. Experiment with various types of cheese for a little variation, but this recipe will quickly become a favorite.

Ingredients

4 tablespoons flour

½ teaspoon baking powder

¼ teaspoon salt

1 tablespoon butter

3 tablespoons milk

1 tablespoon bacon

2 tablespoons cheddar cheese, grated

Instructions

Add the flour, salt and baking powder into a mug and mix together. Add in the butter and combine. Add the milk, cheese and bacon into the mug and mix again. Cook in the microwave for 1 minute 30 seconds and serve.

Cherry Mug Cake

This goes perfectly with a little whipped cream and additional cherries or cherry jam poured over the top. This feels like a real summery indulgence, but you will want to make it throughout the year!

Ingredients

3 tablespoons flour

2 tablespoons butter

2 tablespoons sugar

2 tablespoons milk

¼ teaspoon baking powder

1 egg

½ teaspoon vanilla

1 tablespoon cherry jam

1 teaspoon cream

Topping

Whipped cream

Cherry jam

Vanilla ice-cream

Instructions

Melt the butter in the microwave for about 20 seconds in a mug. Add the egg, vanilla and milk into the mug and mix together. Add the flour, sugar and baking powder into the mug and mix again. Fold in the jam. Add to the microwave for 1 minute 30 seconds and serve with a topping of whipped cream with jam poured over the top or perhaps with some vanilla ice-cream.

Choc Chip Cookie Dough Mug Cake

An instant favorite with the younger members of the family in particular, this mug cake always proves a winner. Mix up your choice of chocolate chips or combine different flavors to find the perfect combination.

Ingredients

1 tablespoon butter

1 egg

3 tablespoons flour

¼ teaspoon vanilla

1 tablespoon sugar, brown

¼ teaspoon baking powder

3 tablespoons milk

1 tablespoon chocolate chips, semisweet

Instructions

Add the butter to a mug and melt in the microwave for 20 seconds. Add in the egg and whisk. Add the milk, flour, vanilla, sugar and baking powder and mix well. Fold in most of the chocolate chips. Add a few chips to the surface of the dough. Cook in the microwave for 1 minute 30 seconds and serve.

Chocolate Almond Mug Cake

Ingredients

3 tablespoons almond flour

2 tablespoons cocoa powder, unsweetened

½ teaspoon baking powder

1 egg

1 tablespoon honey

1 tablespoon milk

1 tablespoon olive oil

½ teaspoon vanilla

1 teaspoon almond extract

Powdered sugar for topping

Instructions

Add the almond flour, cocoa powder and baking powder into a mug and mix. Add in the egg, honey, oil, milk, almond extract and vanilla and whisk together. Cook in the microwave for 1 minute 30 seconds and sprinkle a little powdered sugar over the top before serving.

Chocolate Mug Cake

The essential mug cake might simply be a chocolate mug cake. The chocolate chips melt beautifully here providing a molten treat of chocolatey goodness whenever they are encountered. Complement with a little vanilla ice-cream for an indulgent treat just for one.

Ingredients

3 tablespoons flour

2 tablespoons sugar

2 tablespoons cocoa

¼ teaspoon baking powder

¼ teaspoon salt

3 tablespoons milk

1 tablespoon oil

¼ teaspoon vanilla

1 tablespoon chocolate chips

2 strawberries, chopped

Instructions

Add the dry ingredients into your mug. Add in the milk, oil and vanilla and mix well. Spoon in the chocolate chips. Add to the microwave and cook for 1 minute and 30 seconds. Add the strawberries on top and enjoy by itself or with a little cream or vanilla ice-cream.

Chocolate Orange Mug Cake

Chocolate and orange is a classic combination and this recipe is no exception. A little extra time is needed for the orange zest, but it is worth the additional effort for this classic mug cake.

Ingredients

4 tablespoons flour

¼ teaspoon baking powder

1 tablespoon butter

1 egg

3 tablespoons orange juice

2 tablespoons orange zest

¼ cup sugar

¼ teaspoon salt

¼ cup chocolate chips

½ teaspoon vanilla

Topping

2 tablespoons confectioners' sugar

½ teaspoon water

Instructions

Melt the butter in the microwave for about 20 seconds in a mug. Add the flour, baking powder, sugar and salt together into the mug and mix. Add in the egg, orange juice, zest, vanilla and mix again. Fold in the chocolate chips and cook in the microwave for 1 minute 40 seconds.

Mix the confectioners' sugar with water until the desired consistency is reached and add to the top of the cake. Grate a little more orange zest over the top and serve.

Chocolate Peanut Butter Mug Cake

Simple and quick to make, but one that will always prove a hit. Add a fraction more peanut butter if you want the extra peanut taste as well.

Ingredients

3 tablespoons flour

¼ teaspoon baking powder

2 tablespoons butter

1 tablespoon peanut butter

2 tablespoons cocoa powder

Pinch of salt

1 ½ tablespoons sugar

3 tablespoons milk

1 tablespoon chocolate chips

Instructions

Melt the butter in your mug in the microwave for 20 seconds. Add in the flour, sugar, cocoa powder, baking powder and salt and mix. Add the milk and peanut butter and mix again. Fold in the chocolate chips. Add to the microwave for 1 minute 30 seconds and serve.

Chocolate Zucchini Mug Cake

Ingredients

3 tablespoons flour

1 tablespoon cocoa powder, unsweetened

½ teaspoon baking powder

Pinch of salt

1 tablespoon sugar, brown

3 tablespoons milk

½ teaspoon vanilla

3 tablespoons zucchini, shredded

2 tablespoons chocolate chips, semisweet

Instructions

Shred the zucchini and remove any excess moisture. Add in all but the final two ingredients into your mug and mix well. Fold in the zucchini and most of the chocolate chips and mix well. Sprinkle the remaining few chocolate chips onto the top of the mug. Cook in the microwave for 1 minute 20 seconds and serve.

Cinnamon Mug Cake

This is amazing with a cup of steaming coffee and book by your side. The perfect way to while away half an hour with a lovely treat.

Ingredients

1 tablespoon butter

1 egg

3 tablespoons flour

½ teaspoon vanilla

¼ teaspoon baking powder

1 tablespoon sugar

¼ teaspoon baking powder

3 tablespoons milk

½ teaspoon cinnamon

Topping

Cinnamon Sugar

Instructions

Melt the butter in a mug for 20 seconds. Add the egg and whisk. Add in the remaining ingredients and mix well. Cook in the microwave for 1 minute 30 seconds. Sprinkle cinnamon sugar over the top of the mug cake and serve.

Coconut Mug Cake

Ingredients

1 tablespoon butter

1 egg

3 tablespoons all-purpose flour

½ teaspoon vanilla

1 tablespoon sugar

¼ teaspoon baking powder

3 tablespoons coconut milk

1 tablespoon shredded coconut

Instructions

Melt the butter in a mug for 20 seconds. Add the egg and whisk. Add the vanilla and coconut milk, followed by the flour, baking powder and sugar. Mix well. Fold in the shredded coconut. Cook in the microwave for 1 minute 30 seconds, top with any remaining shredded coconut flakes you have and serve.

Coffee Mug Cake

Ingredients

3 tablespoons flour

2 tablespoons butter

¼ teaspoon baking powder

3 tablespoons milk

2 tablespoons sugar

½ teaspoon cinnamon

½ teaspoon vanilla

Topping

1 tablespoon butter

1 ½ tablespoons brown sugar

1 tablespoon flour

Pinch of cinnamon

Instructions

Melt the butter in the microwave for about 20 seconds in a mug. Add the flour, sugar, cinnamon, and baking powder to the mug and mix. Add in the milk and vanilla and mix again. Add to the microwave for 1 minute 30 seconds. Add all the ingredients for the topping to a bowl and mix into crumbs. Add the topping to the mug cake once it is removed from the microwave and serve.

Cookies and Cream Mug Cake

Yes, this is rather indulgent but it tastes so good! The kids will adore this recipe with its combination of cookies and cake for a special afternoon treat.

Ingredients

1 tablespoon butter

1 egg

3 tablespoons milk

½ teaspoon vanilla

1 tablespoon sugar

3 tablespoons flour

Pinch of salt

½ teaspoon baking powder

2 tablespoons crushed Oreo cookies

Instructions

Melt the butter in a mug in the microwave for 20 seconds. Add the egg, milk and vanilla and whisk. Add the flour, sugar, salt, baking powder and cookies and mix well. Cook in the microwave for 1 minute 30 seconds and top with whipped cream.

Doughnut Mug Cake

A doughnut in a mug? Yes! This is a simple recipe and you can use any jam you like to create that beautiful doughnut taste and smell in just a couple of minutes.

Ingredients

1 tablespoon butter

1 egg

3 tablespoons all-purpose flour

2 tablespoon sugar

¼ teaspoon baking powder

2 tablespoons milk

½ teaspoon cinnamon

½ teaspoon nutmeg

1 tablespoon jam (your choice)

Cinnamon sugar

Instructions

Melt the butter in a mug for 20 seconds. Add in the egg and whisk. Add in the flour, sugar, baking powder, milk, nutmeg and cinnamon and mix well. Remove half the mixture to another bowl and add the jam to the mug. Place the other half back into the mug and cook in the microwave for 1 minute and 30 seconds. Sprinkle with cinnamon sugar before serving.

Eggnog Mug Cake

Eggnog is a great part of the holidays and serving these to guests in little mugs is a fun, light-hearted touch that will both taste delicious and be a great talking point.

Ingredients

4 tablespoons flour

2 tablespoons sugar

½ teaspoon baking powder

¼ teaspoon cinnamon

½ teaspoon vanilla

3 tablespoons eggnog

Whipped cream for topping

Instructions

Add the flour, sugar, baking powder and cinnamon to a mug and mix. Add the vanilla and eggnog and mix well. Cook in the microwave for 1 minute 30 seconds. Remove to cool slightly, add some whipped cream and serve.

French Toast Mug Cake

If you have any leftover bread lying around, this mug cake will make a perfect breakfast treat to set you up for the day.

Ingredients

1 tablespoon butter

2 slices of bread, chopped into pieces

3 tablespoons milk

½ teaspoon cinnamon

½ teaspoon vanilla

1 egg

2 teaspoons maple syrup

Topping

Any chopped fruit or nut goes well

Instructions

Melt the butter in a mug in the microwave for 20 seconds. Cut the bread into small, even pieces. Add the egg, milk, cinnamon, vanilla and maple into the mug and whisk. Add in the pieces of bread, ensuring they are all fully soaked in the egg and milk mixture. Allow the bread a minute or two resting in the mug. Add to the microwave for 1 minute 30 seconds. Remove, add your toppings of choice and serve.

Funfetti Mug Cake

This is so joyous and fun, it's impossible to imagine it not being a huge success in any household. If you have children, they will love admiring the finished creation almost as much as they will eating it.

Ingredients

4 tablespoons flour

2 tablespoons sugar

½ teaspoon baking powder

3 tablespoons milk

½ teaspoon vanilla

2 teaspoons oil

2 teaspoons sprinkles

Instructions

Add the flour, sugar, baking powder and 1 teaspoon of sprinkles into a mug and mix well. Add in the milk, vanilla and oil and whisk together. Add the remaining sprinkles to the top of the mug cake. Cook in the microwave for 1 minute 30 seconds. Allow to cool slightly and serve with vanilla ice cream or whipped cream.

Guinness Mug Cake

It does say mug cake in the title, but this might be one recipe you should make in a glass – a beer glass to be more precise. These mug cakes both look and taste amazing when served to guests for any party.

Ingredients

1 tablespoon butter

4 tablespoons flour

¼ teaspoon baking powder

Pinch of salt

2 tablespoons sugar

1 tablespoon cocoa powder, unsweetened

4 tablespoons Guinness

1 tablespoon chocolate chips, semisweet

Topping

Whipped Cream

Instructions

Melt the butter in a mug for 20 seconds. Add the Guinness into the mug, followed by the flour, baking powder, salt, sugar, cocoa powder and mix well. Fold in the chocolate chips. Cook in the microwave for 1 minute and 10 seconds. Remove and cover with whipped cream to create the perfect Guinness look and serve.

Honey Mug Cake

Ingredients

2 ½ tablespoons butter

2 tablespoons honey

½ teaspoon vanilla

1 egg

2 tablespoons sugar

¼ teaspoon baking powder

4 tablespoons flour

Pinch of salt

Instructions

Melt the butter in a mug in a microwave until runny. Add in the egg, vanilla and honey and beat well. Add in the remaining dry ingredients and beat again. Cook in the microwave for 1 minute and 30 seconds. Remove from the oven and drizzle a little honey over the top to serve.

Ice Cream Mug Cake

For sheer simplicity combined with taste, this recipe of only three ingredients is hard to beat. Mix it up by changing your ice-cream of choice, but it's a winner every time from faithful vanilla to the more exotic flavors.

Ingredients

4 tablespoons flour

½ teaspoon baking powder

½ cup ice-cream (your choice)

Instructions

Add the flour, baking powder and melted ice cream into a mug. Cook in the microwave for 1 minute 30 seconds. Remove and serve with vanilla ice-cream on the side.

Lemon Mug Cake

Ingredients

4 tablespoons flour

¼ teaspoon baking powder

1 tablespoon butter

1 egg

3 tablespoons lemon juice

¼ cup sugar

1 teaspoon lemon juice for topping

Instructions

Melt the butter in the microwave for about 20 seconds in a mug. Add the flour, sugar and baking powder to the mug and mix together. Add in the egg and lemon juice and mix again. Add to the microwave and cook for 1 minute and 30 seconds. Remove from the microwave and pour on a little extra lemon juice as an optional topping.

Matcha Mug Cake

This is perfect for a single serving and I just love the color every time almost as much as the taste.

Ingredients

4 tablespoons flour

1 tablespoon sugar

¼ teaspoon baking powder

1 teaspoon matcha powder

3 tablespoons milk

2 teaspoons oil

Instructions

Add the flour, sugar, baking powder and matcha powder into a mug and mix well. Add in the milk and oil and whisk together. Cook in the microwave for 1 minute 30 seconds. Allow to cool slightly and serve.

Mint Chocolate Mug Cake

Ingredients

1 tablespoon butter

1 egg

3 tablespoons flour

2 tablespoons sugar

2 tablespoons cocoa

¼ teaspoon baking powder

Pinch of salt

3 tablespoons milk

½ teaspoon peppermint extract

½ teaspoon vanilla

1 tablespoon chocolate chips

Instructions

Melt the butter in a mug in the microwave for 20 seconds. Add the egg, milk, vanilla and peppermint extracts and whisk together. Add the flour, sugar, cocoa powder, baking powder and salt and mix together. Fold in the chocolate chips. Cook in the microwave for 1 minute 30 seconds, allow to cool slightly and serve.

Mocha Mug Cake

The coffee flavor works well with this recipe and you can add a little more coffee granules to increase the strength. Unsurprisingly, this goes absolutely perfectly with a steaming cup of coffee by your side.

Ingredients

1 tablespoon butter

1 egg

3 tablespoons flour

½ teaspoon vanilla

1 tablespoon sugar, brown

¼ teaspoon baking powder

2 tablespoons milk

2 tablespoons water

1 tablespoon cocoa powder

1 teaspoon instant coffee granules

Instructions

Add the butter to a mug and melt in the microwave for 20 seconds. Add an egg and whisk. Add the milk, water, vanilla and coffee granules and mix. Add in the flour, baking powder, sugar and cocoa powder and mix.

Cook in the microwave for 1 minute and 30 seconds. Add a little whipped cream and cocoa powder over the top and serve.

Nutella Indulgence Mug Cake

Yes, it's very rich. And very indulgent. Perhaps this might not be one you make every day, but you will want to! Absolutely delicious, this is a little slice of heaven in mug-form which has the added bonus of being super easy to make.

Ingredients

4 tablespoons flour

¼ teaspoon baking powder

2 tablespoons milk

4 tablespoons Nutella

1 tablespoon cocoa powder, unsweetened

Instructions

If the Nutella is not quite runny, then microwave it just for a few seconds to soften it in your mug. Add in the rest of the ingredients and mix well. Cook in the microwave for 1 minute and 10 seconds and remove. Serve and enjoy.

Oatmeal and Raisin Mug Cake

Ingredients

2 tablespoons oatmeal

2 tablespoons flour

¼ teaspoon baking powder

2 tablespoons raisins

1 egg

3 tablespoons milk

1 tablespoon honey

2 tablespoons sugar, brown

½ teaspoon cinnamon

Instructions

Add the egg, milk and honey into a mug and whisk together. Add in the flour, oats, baking powder, cinnamon and sugar and mix well. Fold in the raisins. Cook in the microwave for 1 minute 30 seconds and serve.

Peach Mug Cake

A lovely fresh peach adds a little extra to this mug cake, but tinned peaches will do a great job as well. Use the remaining liquid to pour over the top of the cooked mug cake just before serving.

Ingredients

1 tablespoon butter

3 tablespoons flour

¼ teaspoon baking powder

¼ teaspoon cinnamon

Pinch of salt

1 tablespoon sugar, brown

1 egg

2 tablespoons milk

½ cup peaches, chopped

1 teaspoon walnuts, chopped

Instructions

Melt the butter in a mug in a microwave for 20 seconds. Add in the egg and whisk. Add in the milk and whisk again. Add the flour, baking powder, sugar, cinnamon and salt and mix well. Fold in the cut peaches and walnuts. Cook in the microwave for 1 minute 40 seconds. Sprinkle with any remaining peach juice you may have and serve with some whipped cream or ice-cream.

Peanut Butter and Jelly Mug Cake

This is always a huge hit and it's one the entire family can watch once and make forever after. Stock up on the ingredients!

Ingredients

1 tablespoon butter

1 egg

2 tablespoons milk

½ teaspoon vanilla

2 tablespoons sugar, brown

4 tablespoons flour

¼ teaspoon baking powder

1 tablespoon peanut butter

1 tablespoon jam

Instructions

Melt the butter in the microwave for 20 seconds. Add the egg, milk and vanilla and whisk together. Add in the flour, sugar and baking powder and mix again. Remove half the mixture to a different bowl and add the peanut butter and jam onto the first half. Pour the other half back over the top of the peanut butter and jam. Cook in the microwave for 1 minute 30 seconds and serve.

Pear and Almond Mug Cake

The delicate flavor of pear goes beautifully with almond in this mug cake which always smells as good as it tastes.

Ingredients

1 pear, peeled and diced

1 tablespoon butter

2 tablespoons sugar

3 tablespoons milk

½ teaspoon vanilla

4 tablespoons flour

½ teaspoon baking powder

1 tablespoon almonds, flaked

Instructions

Cook the pear in the microwave for 1 minute and drain off any liquid before dicing. Add the butter to a mug and melt in the microwave for 20 seconds. Add in the remaining ingredients and mix well. Fold in the pear. Cook in the microwave for 1 minute 30 seconds and serve.

Pecan Chocolate Chip Mug Cake

You can make this without the choc chips of course, however I prefer it this way. Try both and decide for yourself!

Ingredients

4 tablespoons flour

¼ teaspoon baking powder

½ teaspoon vanilla

1 tablespoon chocolate chips

1 egg

2 tablespoons pecans, chopped

3 tablespoons maple syrup

Instructions

Add the egg into a mug and whisk. Add in the vanilla and maple syrup and whisk again. Add in the flour and baking powder and mix. Fold in the pecans and chocolate chips. Cook in the microwave for 1 minute and 30 seconds. Remove from the microwave and add a little maple syrup over the top before serving.

Pizza Mug

Pizza in a mug? Absolutely yes and it tastes beautiful. If you need an immediate pizza hit, then this mug is perfect and takes 2 minutes!

Ingredients

4 tablespoons flour

¼ teaspoon baking powder

Pinch of salt

½ teaspoon oregano

3 tablespoons milk

1 tablespoon olive oil

1 tablespoon marinara sauce

1 tablespoon mozzarella, shredded

10 – 12 mini pepperoni slices

Instructions

Add the flour, baking powder, salt and oregano into a mug and whisk. Add the milk and oil and whisk together. Add in the marinara sauce, followed by the mozzarella and the majority of the pepperoni slices before mixing again. Place the remaining mini pepperoni slices over the top of the mug. Cook in the microwave for 1 minute 20 seconds. Let it cool slightly and serve warm.

Pumpkin Mug Cake

A little slice of Thanksgiving that you can make easily throughout the year!

Ingredients

4 tablespoons flour

¼ teaspoon baking powder

2 tablespoons sugar

¼ teaspoon cinnamon

½ teaspoon pumpkin spice

2 tablespoons pumpkin puree

2 tablespoons milk

Whipped cream for topping

Instructions

Add the flour, baking powder, sugar, cinnamon and pumpkin spice into a large mug. Add the milk with the pumpkin puree and mix well. Cook in the microwave for 1 minute and 30 seconds. Remove to cool slightly before adding the whipped cream as an optional topping.

Rainbow Mug Cake

These are simply joyful. I love the colors they produce and they are devoured by both kids and adults alike.

Ingredients

4 tablespoons flour

½ teaspoon baking powder

2 tablespoons butter

1 egg

1 tablespoon sugar

½ teaspoon vanilla

3 tablespoons milk

Food colorings of your choice

Instructions

Add the egg to a mug and whisk. Add in the flour, baking powder, sugar, butter, vanilla and milk. Mix well and separate the batter into a different bowl for each color. Add a couple of drops of the food colorings to each bowl and gently mix. Add the various batches back into your mug alternating between the colors. Cook in the microwave for 1 minute and 10 seconds and serve.

Raspberry Mug Cake

Use frozen or fresh raspberries for a lovely, light mug cake. You can add a few chocolate chips as well if you like.

Ingredients

1 tablespoon butter

4 tablespoons flour

¼ teaspoon baking powder

½ teaspoon vanilla

1 tablespoon sugar

1 egg

2 tablespoons milk

6 raspberries

Instructions

Melt the butter in a mug for 20 seconds. Add the egg, milk and vanilla and whisk together. Add in the flour, sugar and baking powder. Fold in the raspberries and add to the microwave. Cook for 1 minute and 30 seconds and add a little powdered sugar over the top before serving.

Red Velvet Mug Cake

These are so good for Valentine's Day. What could be more romantic than a mug each of lovely Red Velvet Cake? So good, I make it throughout the year as I am sure you will too.

Ingredients

4 tablespoons flour

¼ teaspoon baking powder

2 tablespoons cocoa powder

2 tablespoons sugar

2 tablespoons vegetable oil

3 tablespoons buttermilk

1 egg

1 teaspoon vanilla

½ teaspoon red dye food coloring

Instructions

Add the egg into your mug and whisk. Add in the vanilla, sugar and buttermilk. Add in the flour, baking powder and cocoa powder and mix together. Add the vegetable oil and food coloring and mix again. Cook in the microwave for 1 minute and 30 seconds. Sprinkle a little sugar over the top and serve.

Rum Mug Cake

Any type of rum will work with this recipe. I tend to opt for a dark rum but do experiment yourself with different flavors to find your personal favorite.

Ingredients

1 tablespoon butter

4 tablespoons flour

½ teaspoon baking powder

1 egg

2 tablespoons sugar, brown

¼ teaspoon nutmeg

¼ teaspoon cinnamon

3 tablespoons milk

½ teaspoon vanilla

2 tablespoons rum

Instructions

Add the butter to a mug and melt for 20 seconds in the microwave. Add an egg and whisk together. Add in the flour, baking powder, nutmeg, cinnamon, sugar, milk, vanilla and rum and mix well. Add to the microwave and cook for 1 minute 30 seconds. Remove and serve.

S'Mores Mug Cake

Ingredients

1 egg

3 tablespoons flour

¼ teaspoon baking powder

1 tablespoon sugar

2 tablespoons cocoa powder, unsweetened

1 tablespoon oil

3 tablespoons milk

2 tablespoons graham crackers, crushed

3 or 4 marshmallows

Instructions

Add the egg, flour, sugar, baking powder, cocoa powder, oil and milk into a mug and mix well. Add the crackers onto the top of the mug and as many marshmallows as you like on the top of the crackers. Cook in the microwave for 1 minute and serve.

Salted Caramel Mug Cake

Ingredients

1 egg

1 tablespoon butter

4 tablespoons flour

3 tablespoons milk

½ teaspoon vanilla

2 tablespoons sugar, brown

1 tablespoon cocoa powder, unsweetened

1 tablespoon chocolate chips, semisweet

Pinch of salt

2 tablespoons salted caramel

Instructions

Melt the butter in the microwave for 20 seconds. Add in the egg, milk and vanilla and whisk together. Add in the remaining ingredients apart from the caramel and mix well. Fold in the salted caramel and mix again. Cook in the microwave for 1 minute 10 seconds and serve with vanilla ice cream.

Strawberries with Cream Mug Cake

Ingredients

4 tablespoons flour

¼ teaspoon baking powder

2 tablespoons sugar

½ teaspoon vanilla

1 egg

2 tablespoons strawberries, chopped

2 tablespoons milk

2 tablespoons oil

Whipped cream for topping

Instructions

Add the egg into a mug and whisk. Add in the vanilla, milk and oil and whisk again. Now add in the flour, baking powder and sugar and mix. Fold in the strawberries. Cook in the microwave for 1 minute and 30 seconds. Remove from the microwave and allow to cool slightly before adding the optional whipped cream topping with a strawberry slice on two on the top.

Triple Chocolate Mug Cake

Just how much chocolate can you squeeze into one mug cake? Quite a lot is the answer with this recipe.

Ingredients

1 tablespoon butter

1 egg

3 tablespoons flour

½ teaspoon baking powder

1 tablespoon cocoa powder, unsweetened

1 tablespoon sugar

½ teaspoon vanilla

3 tablespoons milk

1 tablespoon chocolate chips, semisweet

1 tablespoon white chocolate chips

Optional topping

Powdered sugar

Vanilla ice cream

Instructions

Melt the butter in a mug in the microwave for 30 seconds. Add an egg, milk and vanilla and whisk. Add in the flour, baking powder, cocoa and sugar and mix well. Fold in all the chocolate chips. Cook in the microwave for 1 minute 30 seconds and remove to cool a little. Dust with some powdered sugar and serve with a little whipped cream as a topping or vanilla ice cream on the side (or both).

Vanilla Chai Mug Cake

This might take a little longer than usual as you need to let the chai tea bag fully infuse your water, but the results are worth the wait. A lovely delicate chai flavor that is complemented by the vanilla.

Ingredients

1 vanilla chai tea bag

3 tablespoons flour

2 tablespoons sugar

Pinch of salt

½ teaspoon baking powder

3 tablespoons milk

½ teaspoon vanilla

Instructions

Add 1/3 cup of boiling water to the tea bag in a mug and let it rest for 5 minutes. Add the milk and vanilla and whisk. Add in the flour, sugar, salt and baking powder and mix well. Cook in the microwave for 1 minute 30 seconds and serve.

Vanilla Mug Cake

The simple flavor of vanilla is a personal favorite of mine – I love vanilla ice cream! This cake, with its whole teaspoon of vanilla, smells lovely and will prove a huge hit with any vanilla fan.

Ingredients

4 tablespoons flour

¼ teaspoon baking powder

1 teaspoon vanilla

Pinch of salt

1 tablespoon sugar

½ tablespoon melted butter

3 tablespoons milk

Icing

2 tablespoons powdered sugar

1 tablespoon water

½ teaspoon vanilla

Instructions

Add the butter to a mug and melt in a microwave. Add in the milk and vanilla and mix together. Add in the remaining dry ingredients and mix again. Add to the microwave and bake for 1 minute 30 seconds.

Add the icing ingredients together and mix well. If too thick, you can add a little water or milk. If too runny, add a little more sugar. Drizzle the icing over your mug cake and serve with whatever decorations you like over the top!

White Chocolate and Cranberry Mug Cake

Ingredients

4 tablespoons flour

¼ teaspoon baking powder

½ teaspoon vanilla

2 tablespoons sugar

2 tablespoons milk

1 egg

1 tablespoon cranberries, dried

½ cup white chocolate chips

Instructions

Add the egg to a mug and whisk. Add in the vanilla and milk and whisk again. Add the flour, baking powder and sugar and mix well. Fold in the cranberries and chocolate chips. Cook in the microwave for 1 minute and 30 seconds and serve.

Printed in Great Britain
by Amazon